As a souvenir of a wonderful experience

Ilario

may '98

ANCIENT LAND, ANCESTRAL PLACES

ANCIENT LAND, ANCESTRAL PLACES

Paul Logsdon in the Pueblo Southwest

Essays by Stephen H. Lekson and Rina Swentzell

Photographic text by Catherine M. Cameron

Museum of New Mexico Press ▪ Santa Fe

The publisher gratefully acknowledges the following sources in preparing the illustrations
contained in this volume: *The Architecture and Dendrochronology of Chetro Ketl*, ed. Stephen
H. Lekson (National Park Service, 1983). *Archaeological Investigations at Antelope House*, by
Don P. Morris (National Park Service, 1986). *Great Pueblo Architecture of Chaco Canyon,
New Mexico*, by Stephen H. Lekson (University of New Mexico Press, 1986). *The Outlier
Survey*, by Robert P. Powers, et al. (National Park Survey, 1983). *Pecos Ruins: Geology,
Archaeology, History, Prehistory*, ed. David Grant Noble (School of American Research,
1981). *Pueblo Ruins of the Galisteo Basin, N.M.*, in Archaeological Papers of the American
Museum of Natural History, vol. XV, Part I, by N. C. Nelson (1914). *Reconstructing
Prehistoric Pueblo Societies*, ed. William A. Longacre (University of New Mexico Press,
1970; © School of American Research, Santa Fe). *A Zuni Atlas*, by T. J. Ferguson and
E. Richard Hart (University of Oklahoma, 1985).

The Museum of New Mexico Press is a unit of the State Office of Cultural Affairs.

Manufactured in Korea
10 9 8 7 6 5 4 3 2 1

Project editor: Mary Wachs
Designer: Linda Seals
Cartography and drawings: Deborah Reade
Composition: Gill Sans and Bembo set by Wilsted & Taylor, Oakland

Library of Congress Catalog Card Number: 92–84066
ISBN (CB) 0–89013–245–3; (PB) 0–89013–246–1

Museum of New Mexico Press
P.O. Box 2087
Santa Fe, New Mexico 87504

CONTENTS

PLATES

vi

FOREWORD

At first glance, these landscapes of geometry, earth forms rising from a mesmerizing expanse of arid land and rock, do not look earthly, or not the earth we know. This empty place could more believably be a distant planet, unexplored and uninhabitable. But scrutiny reveals that it is our world, from another time and seen from a place that mortals can inhabit only momentarily. These are the exquisite aerial images of veteran pilot, master photographer, and avocational archaeologist Paul Logsdon (1931–1989).

To see the world as Paul did required more than just the bird's-eye view. He was a pilot of superior skill. Trained in the United States Air Force, he flew many types of aircraft for more than twenty years, choosing retirement in 1976. But he could not retire his love of flying, nor his insatiable delight in the ancient cultural sites of the Southwest, a number of which he both discovered and mapped.

We know more of the genius of southwestern cultures because of Paul's daytime sorties. The archaeologist sees with his trowel and searches the dust for pieces of a forgotten activity. Archaeology is tedious work, the sifting and sorting, mapping and recording. It focuses the imagination on the puzzles of the fragmented past: the sherds, chips, bones, and seeds. How easy to become overwhelmed in the magnitude of the tasks and the enormity of the artifact count.

In place of tedium Paul substituted immense technical challenges and the not inconsiderable problem of cramming his six-foot-plus frame, three camera bodies, and a baker's dozen of lenses into his diminutive Cessna 150, the little single-engine he called his "tall tripod." To catch his subjects at home he frequently arrived at dawn's first light, sometimes after a brief skiff of snow had painted in just a little more contrast in an otherwise monochromatic landscape.

Why did he study sites from the air? What impassioned him to hang precariously over deteriorating piles of rubble, the cold rushing into an open cockpit window? In Paul's words, he tried to tiptoe unobtrusively through the air. He wanted to capture the effect of man on the earth and show the ancient signatures of diverse cultures that ebbed and flowed across the Southwest. He tried, with consistent vision and considerable success, to produce a body of work that captured the spirit of the builders of these ancient places.

I have many favorites, as will you. These towering reconstructed pueblos that render our magnificent southwestern landscape even more impressive are certainly images for posterity. But equally beguiling are the little-known ruins that seem to be returning to the soil all too quickly. I have many times from the ground pondered their silence; from Paul's lofty vantage point I can now marvel at their simplistic intricacy.

These photographs will endure as a testimony to Paul's love of the land and its people. More than ever we need them now. They remind us of our rapidly disappearing past, too-quickly evolving environment, and of a lone, intrepid imagemaker who found just the right perch from which to capture it all.

John E. Lobdell
Placitas, New Mexico

RUINS OF THE FOUR CORNERS, VILLAGES OF THE RIO GRANDE

By Stephen H. Lekson

The best way to see the archaeology of the American Southwest is from the air, several hundred feet above the ground. The tumbled walls and low mounds of rubble—all that remain, after half a millennium or more, of ancestral Pueblo towns and villages—appear random and even chaotic to the hiker, but from above they give way to a geometric regularity that can appear organic, like the growth of a plant or the ramification of a crystal, or artificial and designed. Whatever the nature of the pattern it reveals, the aerial view makes clear an order obscure from the ground.

A high viewpoint also imparts, immediately, the relationship of the ruin to its landscape. It takes days of wandering on the ground to grasp what we see in a single glance from altitude: no ancestral Pueblo ruin or modern Pueblo village was placed "out there" arbitrarily, without profound reference to its setting and surroundings. The criteria for selecting townsites changed from time to time and group to group and today they are elusive, but every ruin and every pueblo has some aspect of place that simultaneously sets it apart from and integrates it into its landscape.

Archaeological eyes are drawn to the unique. What is special or unusual about the location of a ruin? It might be on a low knoll, giving it higher visibility or better drainage; it might be at a constriction of the river bottom, the ideal place for diversion dams to feed the irrigation canals; it might be proximity to a spring. Every place that Pueblo peoples invested with building has, to non-Pueblo eyes, some characteristic, subtle or obvious, that sets it off from its surroundings: "*That's* why they built it there!" We can search for days and months on the ground and not understand; but, from above, the reasons often are instantly clear.

Pueblo people, I think, would turn that non-Pueblo search for cause on its head. It is not the place, per se, that is special, but the place's relationship to and integration within the world around it. From that perspective, every ruin and every pueblo *fits perfectly into* its landscape. This is particularly true from the human, head-high perspective. From the ground, the Hopi village of Walpi extends the rock strata of underlying First Mesa, and Peñasco Blanco is indistinguishable from nearby sandstone outcrops.

Even more than the illusive qualities of local mud and local stone built into land-mimicking forms, pueblos and ruined pueblos are placed within larger cosmological landscapes: sacred mountains, shrines, ancestral ruins, and the plaza at the living village's center are structured in a coherent geography of life and tradition. The plaza may contain a "center place," an unpretentious physical construct that marks the middle of that pueblo's world, but that place is neither unique nor permanent. Various pueblos each have their own "center places," and their origin stories tell us that the "center place" moves. More important by far is the philosophical relationship of the pueblo to its surrounding earth; indeed, the "center place" is defined by that relationship. In this sense—not immediately visible to non-Pueblo eyes, however high their viewpoint—pueblos and pueblo ruins are deeply incorporated into the world around them. They are completely integrated into their landscape.

The relationship of pueblos and ruins to the land defines Pueblo history on even larger scales. To really comprehend the scale of Pueblo history requires not an airplane but a satellite or shuttle. The Pueblo story was played out over a region covering two hundred thousand square miles, a region approximately the size of France. At its heart, geographically and historically, is the Four Corners country, so named for the conjunction of present-day New Mexico, Colorado, Utah, and Arizona.

The Four Corners area was, millions of years ago, a sea, and today its structure is as flat as the seabed it once was. Immensely thick layers of tan and red sandstone and gray shale alternate in the walls of deep-cut canyons and in the steep slopes of mesas. In a few widely scattered places, the jagged plugs of old volcanoes show where molten rock cracked through isolated weak spots in the thousand-feet-thick sandstone bed. Circumscribing the region, mountains push the level strata up in striking pine-forested slopes. There are deep canyons and high mesas, volcanic plugs and encircling mountains, but the Four Corners region itself is predominately flat.

It is an arid land, where rain falls only in brief late-summer thunderstorms, running off the shallow soil and racing down through the canyons. For part of the year it is also a cold land. Half of the moisture comes from snows during winters that can be bitterly cold, sinking into the ground with the gradual melting of spring.

Plants and animals must be adapted to drought. Scrub forests of piñon pine and juniper—trees that live happily in arid conditions—are separated by broad plains of sparse brown desert grasses. Antelope and mule deer, well suited to the desert, are the largest game animals. A few permanent streams cut through the

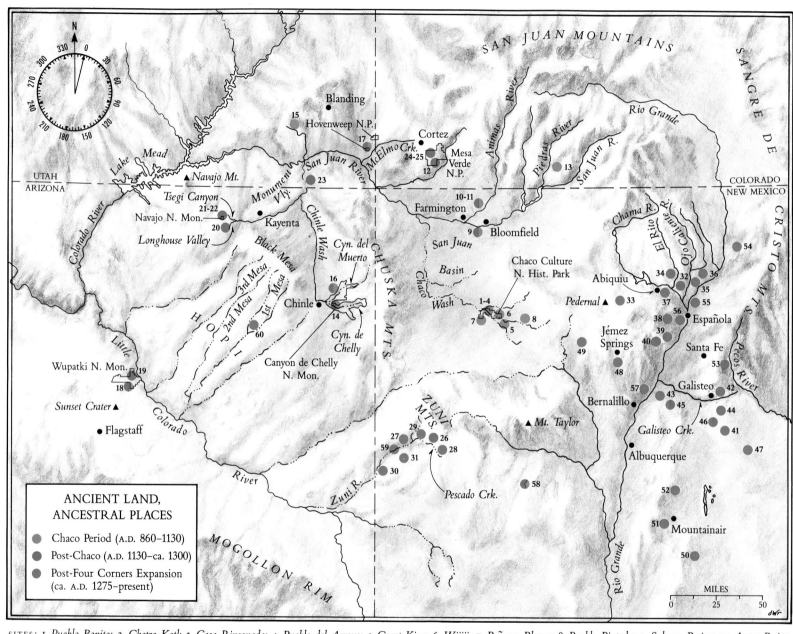

4

ANCIENT LAND,
ANCESTRAL PLACES

● Chaco Period (A.D. 860–1130)

● Post-Chaco (A.D. 1130–ca. 1300)

● Post-Four Corners Expansion
    (ca. A.D. 1275–present)

MILES

0   25   50

SITES: 1 *Pueblo Bonito;* 2 *Chetro Ketl;* 3 *Casa Rinconada;* 4 *Pueblo del Arroyo;* 5 *Great Kiva;* 6 *Wijiji;* 7 *Peñasco Blanco;* 8 *Pueblo Pintado;* 9 *Salmon Ruins;* 10 *Aztec Ruins;* 11 *Aztec Bench;* 12 *Sun Temple, Mummy House;* 13 *Chimney Rock;* 14 *White House;* 15 *Mule Canyon Ruin;* 16 *Antelope House;* 17 *Stronghold House;* 18 *Wupatki Pueblo;* 19 *Wukoki;* 20 *Long House;* 21 *Kiet Siel;* 22 *Scaffold House;* 23 *Poncho House;* 24 *Square Tower House;* 25 *Cliff Palace;* 26 *Cebollita;* 27 *Yellowhouse;* 28 *Atsinna;* 29 *Heshotauthla;* 30 *Hawikuh;* 31 *Kyaki:ma;* 32 *Leaf Water;* 33 *Tsiping;* 34 *Sapawe;* 35 *Posi-Ouinge;* 36 *Hupobi-Ouinge;* 37 *Poshou;* 38 *Puyé;* 39 *Tyuonyi Pueblo;* 40 *Kiva House, Alamo Canyon;* 41 *Pueblo Colorado;* 42 *Las Madres;* 43 *San Lazaro;* 44 *Pueblo Shé;* 45 *Burnt Corn Ruin;* 46 *Comanche Gap;* 47 *Pueblo Largo;* 48 *Guisewa;* 49 *Kwastiyukwa;* 50 *Gran Quivira;* 51 *Abó;* 52 *Quarai;* 53 *Pecos Pueblo;* 54 *Taos Pueblo;* 55 *San Juan Pueblo;* 56 *Santa Clara Pueblo;* 57 *San Felipe Pueblo;* 58 *Acoma Pueblo;* 59 *Zuni Pueblo;* 60 *Hano-Sichomovi-Walpi.*

Four Corners, but, in the past as today, farming depends almost entirely on the undependable late-summer rains.

The northern Rio Grande is the eastern boundary of the Four Corners country. Flat-laid sandstones give way entirely to volcanic rocks. Instead of solitary volcanic plugs, poking up here and there through the plains, complexly intertwined mountain ranges mark the circumferences of gigantic volcanoes. Deep sheets of black lava and gray-white ash, solidified long before humans reached the Southwest, spread out over thousands of square miles. Cutting deeply through the volcanic flows, the Rio Grande gathers up its tributaries, which themselves have cut smaller, steep-sided canyons into the ash and lava flows. To these side canyons—places like the Rio Chama and Rito de los Frijoles—the Pueblo peoples of the Four Corners moved during the twelfth and thirteenth centuries.

They may have been drawn from the west to the Rio Grande, at least in part, by what lay even farther east: the Great Plains. Only a few dozen miles beyond the river, the volcanic land changes grades into the plains, of little use to ancient Pueblo farmers but home to the buffalo, an animal of great interest to peoples who had no domestic sources of meat or hides. Whatever the reasons, Four Corners peoples came to the northern Rio Grande to found the original settlements of Zia, San Ildefonso, Santo Domingo, Santa Clara, Sandia, and the other living towns we know today as the pueblos.

When we think of the pueblos, we think of settlements of great permanence and vast antiquity. Acoma, for example, was a town when Genghis Khan conquered China and King John approved the Magna Carta, but not the Acoma we see today, which was first built about 1650. The Pueblo towns of the northern Rio Grande have long histories, but in archaeological (if not mythic) time, most of them are relatively young. The deeper history lies to the west, in the Four Corners.

The Pueblo peoples of the Rio Grande began hundreds of miles away in the Four Corners country, where no Pueblo people live today. The famous sites of Mesa Verde and Chaco Canyon are their original homes. Today, the Pueblos are separated by time, distance, and—perhaps most importantly—control over their ancestral homes. The great ruins of the Four Corners are in national parks; lesser sites are today on Navajo and Ute Indian lands (neither tribe is related to the Pueblos), on public lands, or are owned by ranchers and farmers. Of ruins developed for public visits, only Puyé on Santa Clara Pueblo lands is owned and administered by Pueblo people. (Other famous ruins, such as Awatovi, Hawikuh, Village of the Great Kivas, and Yellowhouse, are on the lands of various pueblos, but these are not open to the public.)

Even the names we use today are foreign, non-Pueblo. Archaeologists call these sites "Anasazi," a word borrowed from the Navajo peoples who live in the Four Corners today. "Mesa Verde" and "Chaco" are not words in any of the half-dozen languages spoken at different pueblos. "Mesa Verde," of course, is Spanish; "Chaco" is anybody's guess (it is probably either frontier Spanish or mis-copied Navajo). "Cliff Palace" is romantic English, and "Pueblo Bonito" equally romantic Spanish. Yet these places, during the tenth through thirteenth centuries, were the springs of Pueblo life—the Athens and Florence of Pueblo history.

Because they are now sundered, as real estate, from the Pueblos, the connection is not sufficiently obvious for most non-Pueblo people. We prefer to cloak the ruins of the Four Corners in melodrama and mystery. An obsolete (and now largely discarded) Park Service theme, kept alive by a dozen Four Corners chambers of commerce and a growing number of pulp-fiction authors, is the "mystery of the Anasazi—where did they go?" Indeed, it is difficult to find any popular publication on the archaeology of the Four Corners that does not use the words "mystery" and "disappearance."

As recently as 1990, a consortium of government agencies sponsored a "great debate" on this very topic. The title of the verbatim proceedings, published as a popular volume in 1991, at least avoided "mystery" but still couched the "debate" as a mysterious question: *The Anasazi: Why did they leave? Where did they go?* (Southwest Natural and Cultural Heritage Association, Albuquerque). For the panel of Indian and non-Indian authorities who participated, the debate was over before it began: the Anasazi are today's Pueblo peoples, a fact White science has known for almost a century and Pueblo people have known for a good deal longer.

While there is no mystery in the Anasazi, the story of how Mesa Verde and Chaco came to be the modern pueblos is one of real interest and excitement. Pueblo peoples have traditional knowledge of their past in stories that tell how this world and Pueblo life came to be. In these origin stories, Pueblo peoples in various groups and guises moved over landscapes on a scale that can be described correctly as mythic: first in the emergence from other, earlier worlds to this one; and then in peripatetic wanderings over most of the Southwest (and beyond). The Zuni migration story, for example, literally covers all of the Four Corners and dips down into the deserts of southern Arizona and New Mexico. The final station of every origin story is, of course, the current pueblo, whichever it may be.

It would be easy to dismiss the historical content of origin stories as "myth," but that would be more than simply patronizing; even from the most Eurocentric view, it would be wrong. Origin stories contain several kinds of truth, both spiritual and historic. The historic speaks directly to the Western window on the Pueblo past: science and, specifically, archaeology.

Archaeology cannot and should not "confirm" origin stories, any more than any body of traditional knowledge can "confirm" scientific study. The two views are based on incompatible logics and serve entirely different purposes. Origin stories explain, very specifically, how the Pueblo world came to be and how Pueblo people ought to behave within it. Archaeology is one of many noodling paths of insatiable Western curiosity and, insofar as it has a delimitable purpose, it seeks to know the Southwest as yet an element in the much larger global scheme of humanity. These are very different goals.

We tend to discount the historic content of origin stories, in part because of the huge areas they cover, but we should not. European historical traditions comprise "migrations" and wanderings on similar scales (consider the Israelites). Movement of large groups over large distances is a fact of human evolution. The ancestors of Pueblo and other Indian peoples did indeed move over areas that we, in the timid twentieth century, find tremendous. Initially, there was the migration into the New World (really *new*, some ten thousand years ago). That was a long trip, beginning in east central Asia and ending, finally, at Tierra del Fuego, off the southern tip of South America. Along the way, North America was peopled with groups that lived on the land's abundance: wild game and wild plants. In the Southwest, those resources were thin on the ground, so the earliest ancestors of the Pueblo peoples moved in annual rounds covering several hundreds of miles. With increasing population, those peoples eventually exceeded the capabilities of those thin wild resources, and corn, a food well known to the south, was adopted along with other crops. Farming required more time spent in one spot, and ultimately villages assumed a degree of permanence. But millennia of movement undoubtedly had created traditions inimical to a completely sedentary life. Even by the time of Chaco (A.D. 860–1130) and Mesa Verde and the great sites of the Four Corners (ca. A.D. 1080–1300), the ancestral Pueblo people continued to move, frequently and far.

But not so frequently nor so far as in earlier times. While a hunting group first entering the continent might move every week, Pueblo villages of the Four Corners moved every generation. Where a later gathering group, settling into the emerging Southwest, might move hundreds of miles with the changing seasons, Pueblo villages of the Four Corners moved over the hill, into the next valley. How was this so?

Despite the single addition of corn to the economy, the ancestral Pueblo peoples still relied heavily on hunted and gathered wild resources, not the least of which, in the cold Four Corners, was firewood. A compact village of several hundred people—like Cliff Palace or Long House—could make quite a dent in the local game and in certain key plant resources (such as yucca and firewood), making the radius for acquiring these critical resources infeasibly large. At the same time, repeated plantings of corn and other crops would usually lead to diminished yields, through soil exhaustion, constantly increasing pest populations, and cumulatively greater chances of plant disease. After a decade or two, the nest was fouled: the firewood was all gone, the deer were all gone, and the corn was not like it used to be. It was time to move.

Movement of Four Corners Pueblo peoples need not have been far—only to the next nearest unoccupied valley, beyond the range of the exhausted resources. There, the process could begin all over again, leading again to local degradation, renewed movement, and, after a passage of several generations, perhaps a return to the original village site. "Fallow" village sites could regenerate: the game could return, the soil recover, the piñon and juniper regrow. This process worked well as long as the number of villages remained relatively low, and for many centuries it did. In the Four Corners today, there are many thousands of archaeological sites, but only a comparative few were occupied at any one time. There is a lot more archaeology, now, than there were people, then.

The tradition of movement was interrupted only once (or, at least, only once that archaeology has recognized), during the eleventh and early twelfth centuries at Chaco Canyon. The famous ruins of Pueblo Bonito, Chetro Ketl, Peñasco Blanco, and Pueblo Alto are a few of the remarkable buildings crowding this remote, environmentally harsh canyon in northwest New Mexico. Unlike other eleventh- and twelfth-century villages, the big Chaco buildings were not abandoned after a generation. The construction of Pueblo Bonito, for example, took place more or less continuously over two and one-half centuries beginning about

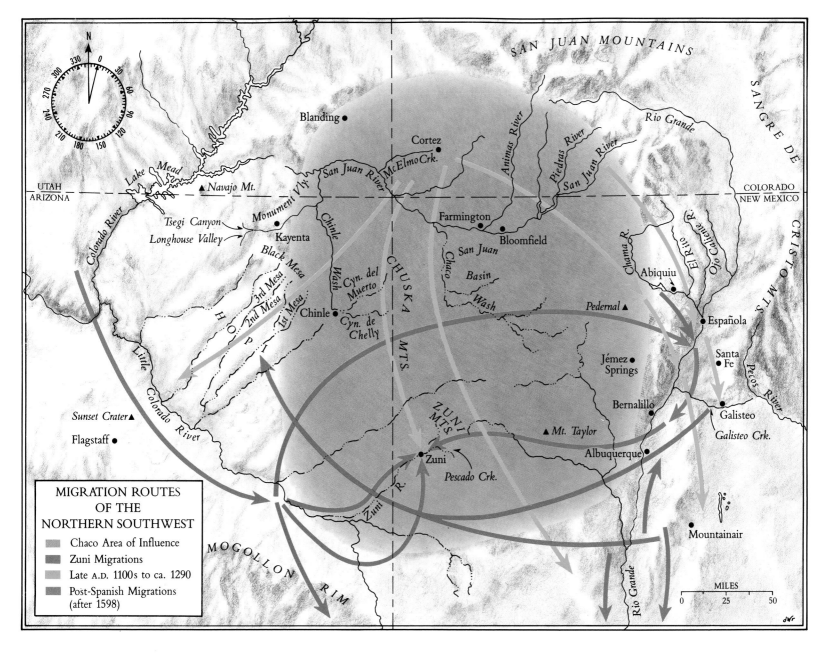

9

N

SAN JUAN MOUNTAINS

SANGRE DE

CRISTO MTS.

Blanding

Cortez

Animas River
Piedras River
Rio Grande

Lake Mead

San Juan River
McElmo Crk.
San Juan River

UTAH
ARIZONA

COLORADO
NEW MEXICO

Colorado River

Navajo Mt.

Monument V'l'y

Chinle

Farmington

Bloomfield

San Juan

Chaco
Wash

Chama R.

El Rio
Ojo Caliente R.

Tsegi Canyon
Longhouse Valley

Kayenta

Black Mesa

Chinle Wash

Basin

Abiquiu

3rd Mesa
2nd Mesa
1st Mesa

Cyn. del
Muerto

Pedernal ▲

Española

HOPI

Chinle

Cyn. de
Chelly

CHUSKA MTS.

Jémez
Springs

Santa
Fe

Little Colorado River

Sunset Crater ▲

Bernalillo

Galisteo

Flagstaff

ZUNI MTS.

▲ Mt. Taylor

Galisteo Crk.

Zuni

Pescado Crk.

Albuquerque

MIGRATION ROUTES
OF THE
NORTHERN SOUTHWEST

Zuni R.

Mountainair

Chaco Area of Influence

Zuni Migrations

Late A.D. 1100s to ca. 1290

Post-Spanish Migrations
(after 1598)

MOGOLLON RIM

Rio Grande

MILES

0   25   50

dVr

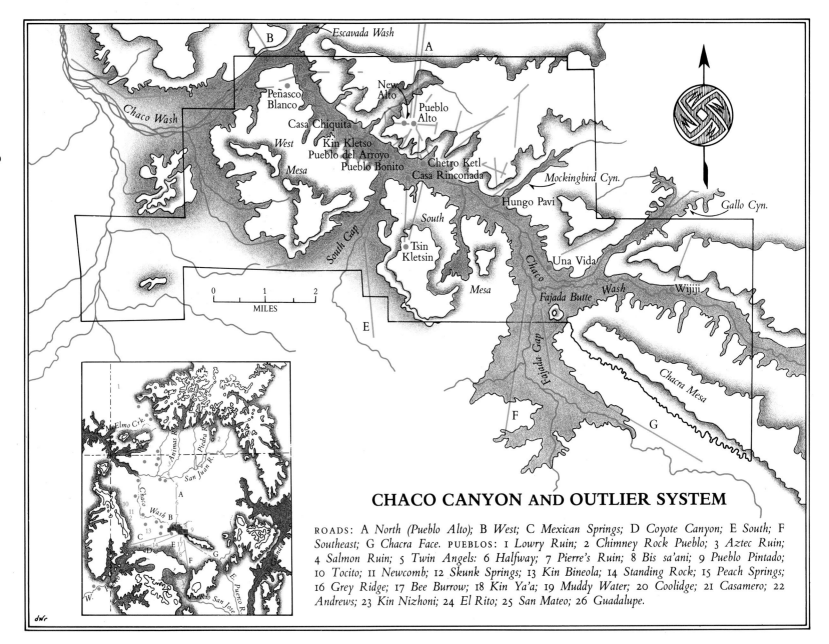

CHACO CANYON AND OUTLIER SYSTEM

ROADS: A *North (Pueblo Alto)*; B *West*; C *Mexican Springs*; D *Coyote Canyon*; E *South*; F *Southeast*; G *Chacra Face*. PUEBLOS: 1 *Lowry Ruin*; 2 *Chimney Rock Pueblo*; 3 *Aztec Ruin*; 4 *Salmon Ruin*; 5 *Twin Angels*: 6 *Halfway*; 7 *Pierre's Ruin*; 8 *Bis sa'ani*; 9 *Pueblo Pintado*; 10 *Tocito*; 11 *Newcomb*; 12 *Skunk Springs*; 13 *Kin Bineola*; 14 *Standing Rock*; 15 *Peach Springs*; 16 *Grey Ridge*; 17 *Bee Burrow*; 18 *Kin Ya'a*; 19 *Muddy Water*; 20 *Coolidge*; 21 *Casamero*; 22 *Andrews*; 23 *Kin Nizhoni*; 24 *El Rito*; 25 *San Mateo*; 26 *Guadalupe.*

A.D. 860; the village continued to be used and maintained for another fifty years. Bonito was not a typical town of its time. In fact, it and the other big Chaco Canyon towns were outstanding exceptions to the rule.

The scale and technology of Chacoan building was also anomalous. The typical habitation of the twelfth century—the kind of home found over all of the Four Corners area—would fit into a single room at Pueblo Bonito. And Pueblo Bonito had eight hundred rooms. It was vastly larger than any other village outside Chaco Canyon, and there were several other comparable structures nearby in the canyon. Everything about Chaco was exceptional, phenomenal, monumental: massively built walls, huge rooms, five stories when a single story was the norm, formal geometries and astronomical alignments, staggering caches of exotic artifacts—these only begin the list of Chacoan anomalies. It was a singular place in its time and in Pueblo prehistory.

All the evidence points to Chaco Canyon being the capital or, at least, center of a vast regional system, with "outlying" Chacoan structures (with the same massive technology and rigid geometry) at places like Aztec, Village of the Great Kivas, and Chimney Rock. Hundreds of "outliers" have now been identified over almost all of the Four Corners area, connected back to the center at Chaco Canyon by an astonishing network of roads, arrow-straight, thirty feet wide, and carefully engineered—road, in a society that had no wheeled vehicles or beasts of burden.

Whatever Chaco Canyon was, it ended after no more than three centuries (not a bad run by modern standards). After about A.D. 1150, construction ceased at Chaco Canyon, but that does not mean that the Four Corners "collapsed." Far from it. The energy of the diminished center moved outward, radiating out to its former peripheries. In the thirteenth and early fourteenth centuries, Mesa Verde, Zuni, the Kayenta area, and the northern Rio Grande—the former edges of the Chacoan regional system—came energetically into their own. This was the era of Cliff Palace and Square Tower House at Mesa Verde, Cebollita at Zuni, Long House in the Kayenta district, and Arroyo Hondo in the northern Rio Grande.

In a few areas, this was also the era of cliff dwellings. Cliff dwellings are so potent an icon of the "vanished Anasazi" that a digression regarding them is justified and, perhaps, required. In novels, in comic strips, in pulp fiction, in movies, in fine-art photography, and—most of all—in the public imagination, cliff dwellings represent, exclusively and sufficiently, the archaeology of the Four Corners. Mesa Verde, with its cliff-dwelling showpieces, is by far the most fa-

PEÑASCO BLANCO, CHACO CULTURE NATIONAL HISTORICAL PARK,
NEW MEXICO (A.D. 900–1130)

mous and most heavily visited archaeological park in the United States. It is easy to understand why. Sheltered under towering sandstone overhangs, sites like Cliff Palace (at Mesa Verde) or Kiet Siel and Betatakin (at Navajo National Monument) remain almost exactly as they were left, 750 years ago.

In fact, all of the famous cliff dwellings have been considerably spruced up by the Park Service and its predecessors, but no matter; they are, indeed, remarkably preserved thanks to the protection of overhanging cliffs. And that is their attraction. They are, today, most extraordinarily intact "ruins" and an unparalleled glimpse of early Pueblo architecture; but they were only a minor element in the life and architecture of their times. A very small percentage of sites were built into cliffs; the vast majority were built out in the open, on terraces, next to mesas, and on low hills, where their stone and mud-mortar walls were exposed to wind and rain and to inevitable collapse. Cliff dwellings were oddities, hidden away in steep canyons of limited agricultural potential. At Mesa Verde, for example, the cliff dwellings were the boondocks; the real cities were out in the plains of the Montezuma Valley (near today's Cortez, Colorado). Built of the same masonry but many, many times larger than the cliff dwellings, these "open" sites are now reduced to rubble mounds—unphotogenic, unappreciated, and unvisited by the public.

A series of very minor villages built into the magnificent walls of Canyon de Chelly warrant a national monument; a nearby open pueblo, ten times larger than the largest Canyon de Chelly cliff dwelling, has been cut through by reservation roads, scored by pipelines, and partially transformed into an historic trading post. No one, outside of the small world of archaeology and the local Navajo, even knows its name. Cliff dwellings are wonderful places, but they tell only a small part of the story.

To return to that story, the post-Chacoan world revived the old, short-term village pattern. Large towns (far bigger than any pre-Chaco formations) were built, occupied, and abandoned in a generation or less, only to be rebuilt a short distance away. But the larger size of each town and the increased total population, together with a perplexing abandonment of the northern Four Corners, brought the older patterns of movement to a halt.

Population typically grows slowly and steadily for centuries, followed by exponential, astronomically explosive growth after a certain threshold of size is reached. This undoubtedly happened in the Four Corners, where post-Chaco towns increased dramatically in number over earlier settlements. The land was filling up. Movement within the Four Corners could no longer assure the resources needed for village life. During the late twelfth century, whole villages began leaving the Mesa Verde area and moving to the all-but-unoccupied Rio Grande, and by A.D. 1300 the whole area was abandoned.

New territories, far to the east and southeast, were colonized, and new ways of using the land evolved. In the Chama Valley, in the Galisteo Basin, on the Pajarito Plateau, at Zuni, and at Hopi, villages were founded which, unlike their predecessors, lasted for multiple generations. Continuity in place was no longer an anomaly, as it was at Chaco Canyon; it was becoming the norm.

But the old patterns of movement were never forgotten. The origin stories reminded Pueblo peoples that they had moved often in the past and that, in some situations, it was still an acceptable option. Towns continued to be abandoned and rebuilt, but more often villages stayed in place or at least in one small locale, and with the coming of Spanish colonists about 1600, the last vestiges of the millennium-old tradition of movement came to an end—almost.

The pueblos appeared, to European eyes, to be permanent settlements; indeed, that is why the conquistadores called them "pueblos." Masonry buildings signified permanence to Europeans, but, in fact, stone and adobe were simply the most convenient materials for an architectural system based on altogether non-European principles. Those principles were never entirely repressed. Even after the Spanish attempted to restrict each pueblo down to land grants four leagues on a side, Pueblo villages still moved, or tried to move. The Salinas pueblos and Galisteo pueblos were abandoned, with some towns relocated a few hundred miles away at Hopi. A Tewa town from the Galisteo still shares First Mesa with two native Hopi villages.

The fluid Pueblo settlement patterns were a major annoyance to the Spanish, who invested a great deal of their time (and a great deal of Pueblo labor) building massive mission churches, only to see the Indian parish evaporate to a new village location. The pueblos at Spanish-period sites like Gran Quivira, Abó, and Pecos are simply rubble mounds today because their builders never intended or planned for them to last forever. Churches, however, were eternal, so they were massively built with impressed Indian labor. As a result, the mission church is often the most impressive monument at abandoned pueblos that once were home to thousands, few of whom had much interest in the church. European notions of permanence operated on a much smaller scale than Pueblo land use. A handful of mission churches stands as lonely monuments to Spanish missionary faith, while

RIO GRANDE GORGE, NEW MEXICO

less conspicuous rubble mounds on a thousand hills and mesas mark, quite literally, the all-pervasive Pueblo relationship to the land.

While the Anasazi of the Four Corners unquestionably became the Pueblo peoples of the Rio Grande, the differing landscapes of those two distinct regions dictated differing lives. The Four Corners is sandstone plains and an era of movement; the Rio Grande is narrow volcanic canyons and increasingly permanent establishment on the land. Changes in Pueblo life reflect both the different landscapes and historical forces in motion more than a thousand years before the Spanish *Entrada*.

After 1600, when Spanish rule was firmly established, ties to the land had a legal, as well as cultural, reality. European colonization and European laws fixed the Pueblos in place, like butterflies pinned to board. If Europe had not arrived, it is entirely possible that the Pueblos would have moved again, back to the Four Corners, the San Juan River and its tributaries—although that direction would be discouraged by some origin stories—or south into what is today Mexico. Who can say? What has not changed through all that time is the Pueblo reverence for the land and for the earth. History has made the focus of Pueblo settlement increasingly specific to one place, one locale; but the dances of the Pueblo people are for all the earth, everywhere.

ANCIENT LAND, ANCESTRAL PLACES

18

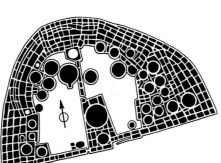

PUEBLO BONITO, CHACO CULTURE
NATIONAL HISTORICAL PARK,
NEW MEXICO (A.D. 860–1130)

One of the largest masonry structures in the prehistoric Southwest,
Pueblo Bonito was built over a period of more than 250 years, from
A.D. 860 to 1100. The structure was
D-shaped with a high, curving back wall; it eventually covered
two acres and was at least five stories tall. It was one of the first
Chacoan Great Houses ever constructed. Its builders experi-
mented with the massive, carefully planned, multistoried construction that became typical of Chacoan Great Houses found
over a wide area of the northern Southwest. Several Great
Houses, including Pueblo Bonito, and scores of smaller buildings
are located in a small area in the center of the canyon often referred to as "downtown Chaco." During the eleventh and early
twelfth centuries, Chaco Canyon was the center of a large regional system that operated over much of the Colorado plateau.
Sites outside the canyon, called outliers, were connected to Chaco
by a system of wide, well-engineered roads.

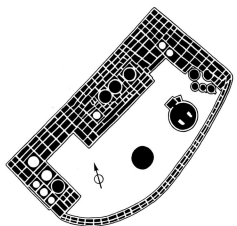

CHETRO KETL, CHACO CULTURE
NATIONAL HISTORICAL PARK,
NEW MEXICO (A.D. 1020–1130)

Chetro Ketl is located in downtown
Chaco Canyon less than one-half
mile east of Pueblo Bonito. Like
Pueblo Bonito, Chetro Ketl is a
Chacoan Great House. D-shaped in
form, its back wall is almost five hundred feet long and may have
been five stories high. A three-story "tower kiva," a rare Chacoan
architectural form, is built into the west side of the central roomblock and may have functioned as a ceremonial signaling location.
East and west roomblocks, connected by an arcing series of small
rooms, create a large plaza in which two Great Kivas were placed.
Outside the arc of rooms were two parallel walls, about six feet
tall and one and one-half feet apart. The narrow space between
the walls apparently was roofed. The function of this structure is
unknown. During excavations of the larger Great Kiva, wall
niches were discovered that contained long strands of black and
white beads up to seventeen feet in length, with pendants of tur-
quoise imported from the mines of Cerrillos, near Santa Fe.

22

PUEBLO BONITO, PUEBLO ALTO ROAD, CHACO CULTURE NATIONAL
HISTORICAL PARK, NEW MEXICO

One of the most distinctive features of the Chacoan system is the
complex of roads that linked Chacoan settlements. These were
not simple trails but wide (sometimes up to forty feet), straight,
carefully engineered roads often curbed with stone. They connected outlying sites with Chaco Canyon, but especially elaborate
roads connected sites within Chaco Canyon. From Pueblo Bonito, a wide staircase led up to the top of the mesa, and from there
a well-defined road led directly to Pueblo Alto. From Chetro
Ketl, the road to Pueblo Alto featured the complex stairway and
staging area at the Talus Unit site.

Pueblo Alto (A.D. 1000–1130) was the terminus for a number
of roads from the north and northeast, including the Great North
Road that linked Salmon Ruins, near Bloomfield, with Chaco
Canyon. Pueblo Alto was distinct among Chacoan Great Houses
in that it was only a single story. The 110 rooms that make up the
E-shaped structure were, however, large and deep. Some archaeologists have speculated that Pueblo Alto may have been a mer-
cantile or religious entry point for travelers to Chaco Canyon.

PUEBLO DEL ARROYO, CHACO CULTURE NATIONAL HISTORICAL PARK,
NEW MEXICO (A.D. 1075–1130)

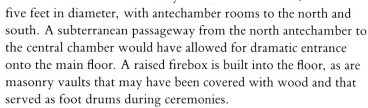

CASA RINCONADA, CHACO CULTURE
NATIONAL HISTORICAL PARK,
NEW MEXICO (A.D. 1070–1130)

Casa Rinconada, a Great Kiva, sits
alone atop a ridge projecting from
the south side of Chaco Canyon.
The structure has a circular central
chamber that is more than sixty-
five feet in diameter, with antechamber rooms to the north and
south. A subterranean passageway from the north antechamber to
the central chamber would have allowed for dramatic entrance
onto the main floor. A raised firebox is built into the floor, as are
masonry vaults that may have been covered with wood and that
served as foot drums during ceremonies.

Within a few hundred yards of Casa Rinconada are ten small
sites that were probably occupied at the same time (seen here to
the right of the Great Kiva). If, as is currently suspected, the large
town sites in Chaco were primarily ceremonial centers, Casa Rinconada probably served as an important center for religious activities for the residents of this portion of the canyon.

GREAT KIVA, CHACO CULTURE NATIONAL HISTORICAL PARK,
NEW MEXICO (A.D. 900–1000?)

This isolated Great Kiva is situated on a low knoll on the south
side of the Chaco Wash about one mile southwest of the site of
Wijiji. Although it has never been excavated, the diameter of the
structure is estimated to be sixty-four feet, slightly less than that
of Casa Rinconada. The Great Kiva has an alcove room on the
northeast side and a midden area to the north and east. Still visible
to the left is an old wagon road that was used during the late nineteenth and early twentieth centuries by Navajo people to haul sup-
plies from the trading post in Chaco Canyon to their hogans on
Chacra Mesa to the south.

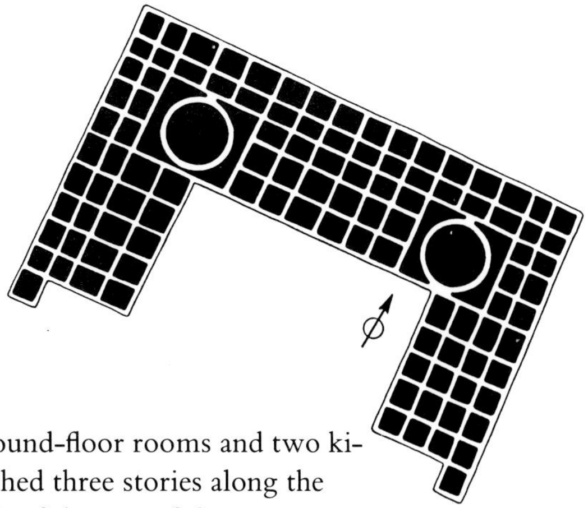

WIJIJI, CHACO CULTURE
NATIONAL HISTORICAL PARK,
NEW MEXICO (A.D. 1110–1130?)

Wijiji is located at the southeast end
of Chaco Canyon, almost six miles
from downtown Chaco. Compared
with other sites in the canyon, it is
a small, compact Great House.
E-shaped with more than ninety ground-floor rooms and two kivas built into the roomblock, it reached three stories along the
back wall and two stories over much of the rest of the structure.
Unlike other Great Houses in Chaco Canyon, Wijiji has no Great
Kiva, no plaza-enclosing arc of rooms, and no trash mound. The
symmetrical layout of the site and extremely uniform room size
suggest that it was built rapidly in a single construction episode
between A.D. 1110 and A.D. 1115. It was erected at the end of the
most intensive period of construction activity of the Chacoan occupation of the canyon. The almost complete lack of potsherds
and other trash suggests that it may never have been actually
occupied.

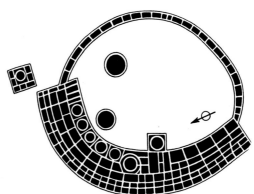

PEÑASCO BLANCO, CHACO CULTURE
NATIONAL HISTORICAL PARK,
NEW MEXICO (A.D. 900–1130)

Peñasco Blanco is located atop a
mesa overlooking the confluence of
the Chaco and Escavada washes, at
the far northwest end of Chaco
Canyon. The original construction
at the site, an arc of masonry rooms three rooms deep and two
stories high, was among the earliest Chacoan construction in the
canyon, dating to the first decades of the A.D. 900s. When completed, the arc was some 590 feet long, five rooms deep, and three
stories high. Later, a one-room-wide arc was added that enclosed
an oval plaza containing two Great Kivas. Outside the site, to the
northwest and south, are two other Great Kivas. Within the
roomblock were seven elevated kivas. Just to the northwest of the
main building, a large artificial platform served as the base for an
L-shaped structure that partly enclosed a circular, subterranean
room. Construction at Peñasco Blanco continued sporadically
over almost two centuries, with the last rooms built about A.D.
1120. A prehistoric road leads northwest from Peñasco Blanco to
Ah-shi-sle-pah Wash less than one mile away, traversing several
rock-cut stairways along its path.

32

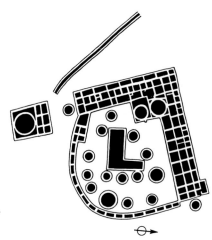

PUEBLO PINTADO, CHACO CULTURE
NATIONAL HISTORICAL PARK,
NEW MEXICO (A.D. 1000–1100)

Pueblo Pintado is situated on a low
terrace south of the Chaco Wash
less than twenty miles east of
downtown Chaco Canyon. This
Chacoan outlier is a conspicuous
landmark in an area of flat terrain. The main structure consisted
of more than 130 rooms and reached three stories in some places.
The structure forms a right angle, and a single curving row of
rooms defines a large plaza area. Four kivas are built into the
structure, while the plaza contains sixteen depressions, many of
which may have been kivas. A prehistoric road enters the site
from the northwest, and another can be traced to the southwest
where it reaches a stone quarry (which may have provided building stone for Pueblo Pintado) and probably continues on to Chaco
Canyon. Like other Chacoan outliers, Pueblo Pintado was surrounded by a community of small domestic structures.

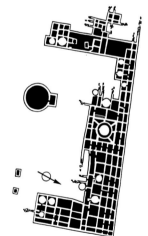

SALMON RUINS, SAN JUAN COUNTY
MUSEUM, NEW MEXICO
(A.D. 1088–1270)

Salmon Ruins is located along the
San Juan River, only a few miles
east of its junction with the Animas
River. Salmon is a Chacoan outlier,
a site built by peoples from, or as-
sociated with, Chaco Canyon, who occupied it from the late eleventh to the mid-twelfth centuries. An E-shaped structure, it was
constructed of well-shaped sandstone slabs and included both an
above-ground tower kiva in the main building and a subterranean
Great Kiva in the plaza. After the Chacoans left, Salmon Ruins
was reoccupied in the A.D. 1200s by peoples with a different, less
precise masonry style, who may have come from the Mesa Verde
area to the north. The settlement was finally abandoned about
A.D. 1270.

AZTEC RUINS, AZTEC NATIONAL
MONUMENT, NEW MEXICO
(A.D. 1100–1250)

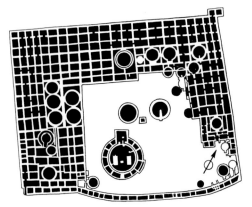

Aztec Ruins is a large complex of prehistoric structures located on the north bank of the Animas River in northwest New Mexico. The name "Aztec" derives from the early settlers' belief that southwestern ruins had been built by peoples from the high civilizations of Mexico. The West Ruin, shown here, is a massive, E-shaped Chacoan outlier, much like Salmon Ruins twelve miles to the south. More than a decade was spent beginning in 1916 excavating and stabilizing the West Ruin, now a national monument. Near the West Ruin are two circular triwall structures, one excavated, the function of which is unknown.

AZTEC BENCH, NEW MEXICO (A.D. 1080–1150)

North of Aztec National Monument is a series of cobble terraces
known as the "Aztec Bench" that contain dozens of prehistoric
sites contemporary with those of the monument. Prehistoric remains on the Aztec Bench are spread across one and one-half
miles and are clearly part of the eleventh- and twelfth-century
Chacoan community at Aztec National Monument. Remains include several multistoried Great Houses, many smaller domestic
structures, a number of Great Kivas, stone quarries, shrines, prehistoric road segments, and earthen platforms.

38

SUN TEMPLE, MUMMY HOUSE, MESA VERDE NATIONAL PARK, COLORADO
(A.D. 1100?–1300)

Sun Temple and Mummy House are part of a large group of cliff
dwellings located at the junction of Cliff Canyon and Fewkes
Canyon near the area's largest spring. The Cliff–Fewkes Canyon
settlements were home to hundreds of people during the A.D.
1200s. Sun Temple's massive D-shaped walls enclose several kivas;
a circular tower is located outside the main structure to the east.
The kivas had subfloor ventilators like those found in Chacoan kivas, suggesting that the structure may have been built by people
from Chaco or by local people following the Chaco style.
Mummy House had twelve rooms and two kivas; some of the
rooms were two and three stories high.

CHIMNEY ROCK, COLORADO (A.D. 1075–1125)

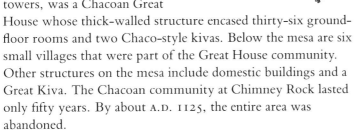

The chimney rocks are tall spires protruding from a high mesa just east of the Piedra River in southwest Colorado. Chimney Rock Pueblo, built at the base of these towers, was a Chacoan Great House whose thick-walled structure encased thirty-six ground-floor rooms and two Chaco-style kivas. Below the mesa are six small villages that were part of the Great House community. Other structures on the mesa include domestic buildings and a Great Kiva. The Chacoan community at Chimney Rock lasted only fifty years. By about A.D. 1125, the entire area was abandoned.

MULE CANYON, UTAH
(LATE A.D. 1000S–EARLY 1100S)

Mule Canyon Ruin occupies a ridge overlooking Mule Canyon in an area of dense piñon-juniper forest about twenty miles southwest of Blanding. It is a small site of a type called a "unit pueblo" that was typical of Anasazi habitation sites during much of early Pueblo prehistory. Excavations by the University of Utah in 1973 uncovered a roomblock consisting of twelve rooms, an oval-shaped tower, and a kiva. The tower and the kiva were connected by a tunnel; another tunnel connected the kiva to the roomblock. The tower may have been a defensive structure or a signaling station.

44

STRONGHOLD HOUSE, HOVENWEEP NATIONAL MONUMENT, UTAH
(A.D. 1100–1300)

Stronghold House is part of a remarkable group of small masonry
structures located at the heads of shallow canyons in southwestern
Colorado and southeastern Utah. It is a two-story structure built
atop a sandstone boulder. Although it resembles a defensive structure, its location below the canyon rim makes for a poor lookout.
Its proximity to a spring and to several other unusual masonry
structures suggests that its purpose was ceremonial.

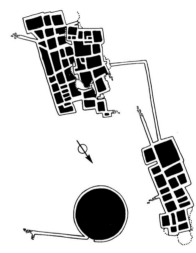

WUPATKI PUEBLO, WUPATKI NATIONAL
MONUMENT, ARIZONA
(A.D. 1100–1190)

With more than one hundred
rooms, Wupatki Pueblo is by far
the largest site in Wupatki National
Monument, a barren area just south
of the Colorado River. The region
was covered with ash from the violent eruption of nearby Sunset
Crater beginning in A.D. 1064. The ash fall created excellent farming conditions over the next 150 years, drawing diverse peoples
from surrounding areas. Like many other sites in the monument,
Wupatki Pueblo was built on a rocky outcrop, incorporating the
outcrop into its masonry walls. In the foreground is a ball court,
one of two community structures found at the site. Ball courts are
typical of the Hohokam area of southern Arizona, making the
Wupatki ball court the northernmost example of this architectural
form. Ball courts may have been used ritualistically, as was the
case in prehistoric Mesoamerica. The other community structure
at Wupatki Pueblo is the "dance plaza," the circular construction
visible at the center of the photograph. It was probably an un-
roofed Great Kiva.

WUKOKI, WUPATKI NATIONAL MONUMENT, ARIZONA (A.D. 1100S)

Like other sites in Wupatki National Monument, Wukoki rises from a knob of red sandstone that sticks out of the sea of black ash left from the eruption of Sunset Crater. A small structure with only three or four ground-floor rooms, Wukoki rises three stories high, its carefully built walls of the same red sandstone as the knob on which it rests. According to a legend told by the Hopi Snake clan, Wukoki was a resting place during Hopi migrations.

CANYON DE CHELLY ROCK ART, ARIZONA

CANYON DEL MUERTO, CANYON DE CHELLY, ARIZONA

Canyon de Chelly and Canyon del Muerto are sandstone canyons with sheer walls soaring more than one thousand feet above their sandy floors. They meet just east of the Navajo settlement of Chinle, Arizona. The canyon bottoms are farmed today by Navajo people. In prehistoric times, from perhaps A.D. 1 to A.D. 1300, the canyons were occupied by the Anasazi. They built masonry villages in overhangs and alcoves; the protected villages today are remarkably preserved. The structures seen here are probably small granaries, built to store produce grown in the canyon below.

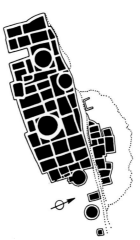

WHITE HOUSE, CANYON DE CHELLY
NATIONAL MONUMENT,
ARIZONA (A.D. 1070–1270?)

White House is located along the
north side of Canyon de Chelly,
about a mile upstream from the
confluence of Canyon de Chelly
and Canyon del Muerto. White
House consists of two structures. At the base of the cliff is a large
masonry pueblo that may have had as many as sixty rooms and
four stories. Just above this structure, in a cave above the canyon
floor, is another group of about twenty rooms. The upper level
could have been reached from the rooftops of the lower structure
when all four stories were in place. The lower structure is massively built in the Chacoan style and has been identified as a Chacoan outlier. Tree-ring dates suggest that it was constructed about
A.D. 1070; there may have been some further construction in the
A.D. 1270s.

DOWOZHIETBITO CANYON, NAVAJO NATIONAL MONUMENT, ARIZONA

TSEGI CANYON, NAVAJO NATIONAL MONUMENT, ARIZONA

The Marsh Pass–Tsegi Canyon area is one of great natural beauty and archaeological importance. Here the high plateau country is cut by deep, narrow canyons and wide valleys. Tsegi is an extensive dendritic canyon system that separates the Shonto Plateau from Skeleton Mesa; Dowozhietbito Canyon is one of its tributaries. At the mouth of Tsegi Canyon is Marsh Pass, a narrow defile that separates the broad Chinle Valley to the northeast from the Long House and Klethla valleys to the southwest. Navajo Mountain rises in the background. The narrow canyons that make up the Tsegi Canyon system were occupied from perhaps 200 B.C. to A.D. 1300. They are best known for the spectacular cliff dwellings built and occupied during the last half of the A.D. 1200s and then rapidly abandoned by A.D. 1300.

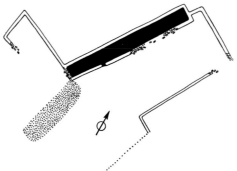

LONG HOUSE, TSEGI CANYON, ARIZONA
(A.D. 1250–1300?)

Long House is perched atop a sand-stone bench on the north side of Long House Valley about fifteen miles southwest of Kayenta. This four-hundred-room pueblo was the largest prehistoric settlement in the valley. The site has been reduced to a rubble mound, although one long, narrow structure (for which the site is named) has standing walls up to ten feet high. A nearby dam and reservoir provided domestic water for the settlement. Long House is one of five "focal sites" in the Long House Valley. Focal sites are surrounded by smaller sites that apparently were part of a community. A number of interesting characteristics distinguish focal sites, including Long House, from the smaller sites: open plaza areas, long, two-story roomblocks, and reservoirs for collecting and storing water. Perhaps most significant, all focal sites are in defensible locations and are visually linked: from each site, all other focal sites can be seen. Tree-ring dates suggest that the standing structure at Long House was built in A.D. 1273–1274.

KIET SIEL, NAVAJO NATIONAL
MONUMENT, ARIZONA
(A.D. 1250–1300)

Kiet Siel is perched in a deep alcove
in the canyon wall of a tributary to
Tsegi Canyon. It was a large cliff
dwelling, with at least 155 rooms,
many courtyards, and six kivas.
Careful tree-ring dating has shown that a few families arrived and
began building the village about A.D. 1250. In the early 1270s, a
number of new families moved to Kiet Siel and the total population reached 150 people. The settlement was short-lived; by A.D.
1300, it was entirely abandoned. Lack of planning and preparation
in the construction of Kiet Siel and its great variety of architectural styles suggest that the inhabitants of the site came from
many different places and had not previously lived together in the
same village.

SCAFFOLD HOUSE, TSEGI CANYON, ARIZONA (A.D. 1273–1300)

The large alcove that holds Scaffold House is on the east side of Tsegi Canyon, just below the mouth of Bubbling Springs Canyon. Here the narrow canyon floor widens enough to permit farming. A seep in front of the site provided water for the village. Scaffold House derives its name from a horizontal platform built in a crevice at the back of the alcove, with beams spanning the length of the crevice, supporting a scaffold or floor with a central hatchway. The scaffold may have served as a lookout but was more likely a secure, dry storage area. Scaffold House had thirty-five rooms, five courtyards, and two kivas strung along the back of the alcove, representing about ten dwellings. Tree-ring dating has determined that building began at the site in A.D. 1273 and the last house was completed in A.D. 1285. Scaffold House was probably abandoned shortly thereafter.

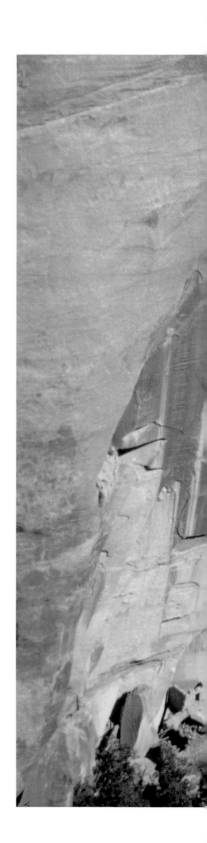

62

PONCHO HOUSE, UTAH (A.D. 1200S)

Poncho House, one of the largest cliff dwellings in Utah, is located in a cove on the east bank of the Chinle River, about ten miles south of its confluence with the San Juan River. The site was first visited in 1875 by photographer William Henry Jackson, a member of the Hayden Geological Survey. Jackson found seventy-five rooms built along a bench below the cliff face. Two groups of rooms were apparent, at the east and west ends of the bench. Several rooms extended to the ceiling of the cave, and one rectangular tower reached three stories. Jackson discovered seven large *ollas* during his visit to the site, presumably storage containers; they were removed and the site vandalized by later visitors. During excavations at Poncho House in 1923, an adult male burial was discovered in a small stone-lined chamber, accompanied by several baskets, ceramic vessels, a bow and arrow, and a large squash. A peculiar poncho-like garment wrapped around the remains suggested a name for the site.

63

MONUMENT VALLEY, ARIZONA

YEI BI CHAI, MONUMENT VALLEY, ARIZONA

SQUARE TOWER HOUSE, MESA VERDE
NATIONAL PARK, COLORADO
(A.D. 1200–1300)

Square Tower House is located on the west side of Chapin Mesa in an alcove beneath a shallow overhang. The Square Tower settlement once contained seventy rooms and seven kivas. Partially intact roofs of two kivas showed a "cribbed" construction that was probably used for kiva roofs at many other sites. The four-story tower contained domestic rooms, once part of a larger terraced structure. A spring was located below Square Tower House and another, larger spring was adjacent to a nearby cliff dwelling to the north. A trail led between the two sites.

CLIFF PALACE, MESA VERDE
NATIONAL PARK, COLORADO
(A.D. 1200–1300)

Cliff Palace, with 220 rooms and
twenty-three kivas, was the largest
of the Mesa Verde cliff dwellings.
The Anasazi built retaining walls
and then leveled the sloping floors
of the rock shelter. The round tower in the center of the site ta-
pers inward. The square tower to the left rises four stories and has
elaborate painted designs on the interior walls. Cliff Palace was
central to the Cliff–Fewkes Canyon community of sites, which
included other, smaller cliff dwellings as well as sites on the mesa
top. It may have housed as many as 250 to 350 people.

CEBOLLITA, ZUNI RESERVATION, NEW MEXICO (A.D. 1250–1300)

Cebollita, also known as "Kluckhohn Ruin" for anthropologist Clyde Kluckhohn, is located on the floor of Togeye Canyon where it joins El Morro Valley. It is constructed of red sandstone. One part of the site consists of a square block of rooms that may have had a central plaza. Northeast of the rectangular structure is a circular structure that may be entirely filled with rooms. The two structures together totaled more than seven hundred rooms. A Great Kiva is located just east of the site.

YELLOWHOUSE, ZUNI RESERVATION,
NEW MEXICO (A.D. 1275–1325)

Yellowhouse is located on a low
ridge just north of Pescado Creek.
The site consists of an L-shaped
masonry structure with two plazas
and at least three kiva depressions.
It has never been excavated. Recent
studies show 243 ground-floor rooms, half with a second story
and some with three stories.

74

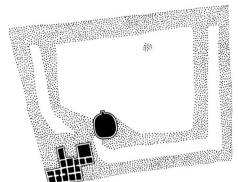

ATSINNA, ZUNI RESERVATION,
NEW MEXICO (A.D. 1275–1350)

Atsinna is located atop El Morro,
an escarpment of rock at the east
end of the Zuni Valley that has become famous for inscriptions
etched there by seventeenth- and
eighteenth-century Spanish explor-
ers and other travelers. The cliffs are covered also with prehistoric
rock art. A large permanent pool of water at the base of El Morro
was an important resource for travelers between Zuni and Acoma,
and many left signs of their passing. "Atsinna" means "where pic-
tures are on the rock," a name that Zuni workmen suggested
when the site was excavated in the 1950s. This ancestral Zuni site
included a rectangular structure with a single central plaza. It may
have had as many as five hundred ground-floor rooms constructed
in blocks two to five rooms deep and from one to three stories
high. Excavations revealed that only plaza-facing rooms had been
used for domestic activities; the others presumably were used for
storage.

HESHOTAUTHLA, ZUNI RESERVATION, NEW MEXICO (A.D. 1275–1375)

Heshotauthla is built at the edge of the Pescado Creek about twelve miles upstream from Zuni Pueblo. Excavations were first conducted here in the late nineteenth century by the Hemenway Expedition, one of the first formal archaeological expeditions in the Southwest. Early maps of the site show an oval pueblo with a central plaza. The dense cluster of rooms that make up the structure reached three stories with a total of almost nine hundred rooms. Outside the outer wall to the south, ovens were found.

ZUNI TWIN BUTTES AND TOWER, ZUNI RESERVATION, NEW MEXICO

KYAKI:MA, ZUNI RESERVATION,
NEW MEXICO (A.D. 1350–1680)

Kyaki:ma was one of the legendary
"Seven Cities of Cibola" sought by
the early Spanish explorers. It is located at the base of Dowa Yalanne
(Corn Mountain), Zuni's sacred
mesa, just east of modern Zuni
Pueblo. It was first occupied during the 1300s and was described
by Spanish explorers in 1581 as a village of seventy-five two- and
three-story houses. By 1680, Spanish priests had added a church.
Upright stone slabs arranged on a cliff just above the site have
been variously described as grave markers, erosion-control features, astronomical markers, or markers for the public entryway
into the pueblo.

LEAF WATER, CHAMA VALLEY,
NEW MEXICO (A.D. 1200S)

The Leaf Water site was built on a
small promontory near the point
where Kapokohu'u Arroyo ("leaf
water" in the Tewa language) enters
the Chama River. Constructed primarily of coursed adobe with some
crude masonry walls, roomblocks were built in a trapezoidal
shape surrounding a central plaza. They were two to four rooms
wide, as much as sixty-five yards long, and may have been two
stories high. Two kivas were found during excavations, one in the
plaza and another under a roomblock. Two pit structures located
in the northeast corner of the site may have been temporary housing used during construction of the main pueblo. Leaf Water was
probably occupied during the second half of the A.D. 1200s, one
of the earlier sites in the Chama Valley.

82

83

TSIPING, CHAMA VALLEY,
NEW MEXICO (A.D. 1300–1400)

Tsiping is perched on a high mesa
that separates Canyones and Pol-
vedera creeks, both tributaries to
the Chama River. The site is close
to Pedernal Peak, the source of a
widely used chipped stone material;
the Tewa name "Tsiping" means "house of the flaking stone
mountain." More than one thousand rooms constructed of volcanic rock were built at the southeast end of the mesa along the
eastern cliff edge. Four plazas were located among the densely
clustered rooms on the mesa top, while other rooms were constructed below, along the face of the cliff. Fifteen kivas were
placed in plazas or outside the roomblocks, including one Great
Kiva. The north end of the mesa was occupied, prehistorically, by
an agricultural field with storage rooms located nearby; a small
reservoir near the site caught rainwater. The defensive location of
Tsiping was enhanced by walls, five feet high and three feet wide,
that protected access to the site.

84

SAPAWE, CHAMA VALLEY,
NEW MEXICO (A.D. 1300–1400)

Sapawe is located on the west bank
of the El Rito Creek about eight
miles upstream from its conjunction with the Chama River. Sapawe
was one of the two or three largest
adobe pueblos in what is now New
Mexico, with more than twenty-five hundred rooms arranged
around seven enclosed plazas, some as large as football fields.

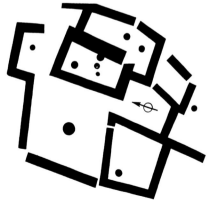

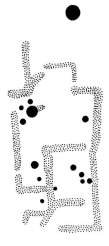

POSI-OUINGE, CHAMA VALLEY,
NEW MEXICO (A.D. 1350–1600)

In Tewa, "Posi-Ouinge" means "greenness pueblo ruin," a reference to the lush growth around the Ojo Caliente springs that bubble out just below the village. Posi, which has never been excavated, was built of adobe and river cobbles with a few slab masonry walls. Ceramics and tree-ring dates suggest that the site was occupied during the late fourteenth, fifteenth, and possibly sixteenth centuries. Its nine roomblocks surround three plazas. Posi may have had more than fourteen hundred ground-floor rooms and risen three stories high. Several small kivas dot the plazas and a single very large kiva is located in the center of the widest plaza. Posi is an important place in Tewa mythology. It was here that the Summer and Winter people came together after their travels, and from here that six groups left to found the six Tewa villages (San Juan, Santa Clara, San Ildefonso, Tesuque, Nambé, Pojoaque) that are vital today.

HUPOBI-OUINGE, CHAMA VALLEY, NEW MEXICO (A.D. 1350–1550)

Hupobi is located along the Rio Ojo Caliente, a tributary to the Chama, about one mile north of the village of Ojo Caliente. "Hupobi-Ouinge" is a Tewa word that means "pueblo ruin of the flower of the one-seeded juniper." Occupied from the fourteenth to the sixteenth century, it was once a multistoried pueblo with perhaps as many as twelve hundred rooms. The remains of prehistoric gardens can still be seen nearby. Numerous petroglyphs have been found on granite boulders northeast of the site. Modern Tewa peoples claim Hupobi as an ancestral village, occupied before they moved to the Rio Grande Valley.

POSHOU, CHAMA VALLEY, NEW MEXICO (A.D. 1400–1500)

CHAMA RIVER WILDERNESS, NEW MEXICO

CHAMA RIVER, NEW MEXICO

92

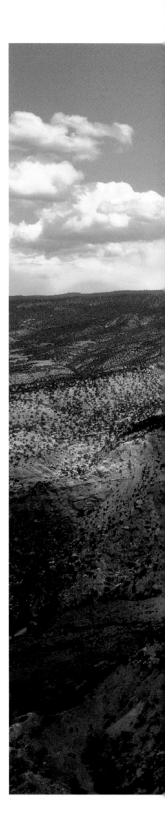

GHOST RANCH, CHAMA RIVER, NEW MEXICO

PUYÉ, PAJARITO PLATEAU,
NEW MEXICO (A.D. 1300S–1500S?)

Puyé is located on Santa Clara
Pueblo land, not far from modern
Santa Clara Pueblo. The site rests
on a narrow mesa of soft volcanic
rock. Excavations, conducted at
Puyé beginning in 1907, uncovered
four massive roomblocks built around a plaza on the mesa top.
Below the edge of the cliff was a long row of "cliff houses" that
included cavates dug into the tuff, some with structures built in
front of them. Multistoried houses of stone were built against the
cliffs. Trails worn deeply into the rock linked the prehistoric Puyé
with nearby communities.

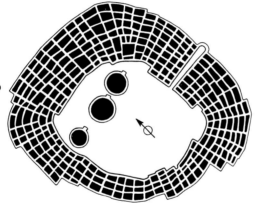

TYUONYI PUEBLO, BANDELIER
NATIONAL MONUMENT, NEW MEXICO
(A.D. 1350–1550?)

Tyuonyi, located in the bottom of
scenic Frijoles Canyon, was excavated around 1910. It was stabilized
by the Civilian Conservation Corps
during the 1930s and is now the
central feature of Bandelier National Monument. The largest of
the ruins in Frijoles Canyon, Tyuonyi was built in an oval shape
with more than 350 rooms; most were a single story, although
many rooms may have been two or even three stories high. The
site was constructed about A.D. 1350 and occupied as late as A.D.
1550. Numerous other residences were built along the adjacent
cliffs, using cavates pecked into the volcanic rock as additional living and storage space. Some archaeologists believe that the circular form of Tyuonyi, with only one entrance to the plaza, made it
a defensive structure. There is evidence of barricades at the plaza
entrance.

ANASAZI GRID FARMS, NORTHERN RIO GRANDE VALLEY

The prehistoric farmers of the arid Southwest needed great ingenuity to produce crops in areas where limited rainfall provided the only source of water. The patterns of stones seen here are the remains of terraces and bordered gardens built by the Anasazi beginning about A.D. 1200. These features were used to prevent soil erosion, enhance solar radiation, and, most importantly, trap the sparse moisture for crops. They were often constructed near villages so that the soil could be enriched by the addition of household refuse. Similar agricultural features can be found throughout the northern Rio Grande region. They are a testament to the intense effort that prehistoric farming required of the native peoples of the Southwest.

KIVA HOUSE, ALAMO CANYON RUIN, BANDELIER NATIONAL
MONUMENT, NEW MEXICO (LATE A.D. 1100S–EARLY 1400S)

Kiva House is located on a talus slope at the mouth of Alamo
Canyon. It was excavated during the 1970s as part of an effort to
salvage sites before they were inundated by Cochiti Reservoir.
The settlement's haphazard layout suggests it may have been built
and occupied over several centuries. Most of the twenty-three
rooms and three kivas that make up the structure are clustered together. An odd string of six rooms that protrudes from the cluster
to the east shows a different architectural style. A kiva probably
associated with this east string of rooms has features that suggest
it was built by immigrants from Mesa Verde.

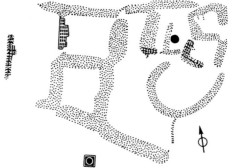

PUEBLO COLORADO, GALISTEO BASIN,
NEW MEXICO (LATE A.D. 1200S–1600)

Pueblo Colorado is one of a number of large prehistoric villages located in the Galisteo Basin, a rolling grassland about twenty miles south of Santa Fe. It is claimed by the Tano Indians of Santo Domingo Pueblo as an ancestral village. They call the ruin "Tze-man Tuo," which may translate, "place where the eagle's claw is inside." Nels Nelson, who excavated the site in the 1910s, called it "Pueblo Colorado" ("red village") because of the red sandstone of which it was constructed. The village may have been first occupied in the late A.D. 1200s. When it was abandoned, before 1600, it consisted of more than fourteen hundred one- and two-story rooms. Incorporated into the site is a C-shaped dam that collected water into a reservoir.

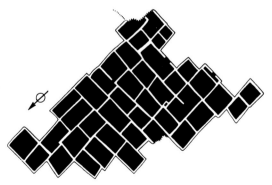

**LAS MADRES, GALISTEO BASIN,
NEW MEXICO (A.D. 1340–1415)**

Las Madres occupies a high, narrow
promontory above the Galisteo
Creek. Excavations in the 1960s revealed a masonry pueblo more than
two hundred feet long and fifty feet
wide. Although only one story
high, the houseblock is built on rolling terrain, creating a terraced
effect. Just across the river is Galisteo Pueblo (also known as Los
Tanos), a large village that may have been partially contemporary
with Las Madres but continued to be occupied into historic times.
Ceramics found at Las Madres are very similar to those from the
Mesa Verde region, suggesting that the site may have been settled
by people from that area.

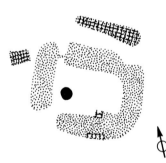

**PUEBLO SAN LAZARO, GALISTEO
BASIN, NEW MEXICO
(LATE A.D. 1200S?–1680)**

Pueblo San Lazaro is divided into
two parts by Arroyo del Chorro, a
tributary to Galisteo Creek. The
prehistoric pueblo is primarily west
of the arroyo, while the historic
pueblo is east. The remains of a small church are associated with
the historic occupation; a nearby reservoir may be prehistoric.
The settlement apparently was abandoned when Coronado passed
by in 1540, but may have been subsequently reoccupied during
the introduction of Spanish missions in the late 1500s. San Lazaro
was abandoned after the Pueblo Revolt of 1680, and its residents
eventually scattered.

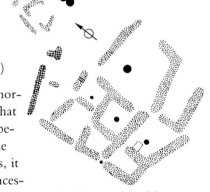

PUEBLO SHÉ, GALISTEO BASIN,
NEW MEXICO (A.D. 1300–1600)

Pueblo Shé is another of the enormous Galisteo Basin pueblos that
was established and occupied between A.D. 1300 and 1600. Like
many of the other area villages, it
was apparently occupied by ances-
tors of the Tano Indians. The settlement had more than fifteen
hundred rooms, built mostly of masonry, in linear and L-shaped
roomblocks surrounding eleven plazas. A large kiva occupied the
easternmost plaza, and smaller depressions suggest kivas in other
plazas. Pueblo Shé included two reservoirs. The reservoir to the
east has been largely destroyed by erosion, but the western reservoir was more than 150 feet long. It was constructed of soil and
sandstone slabs and straddled a small arroyo. Coronado may have
passed Pueblo Shé in 1541; the village was surely abandoned by
the time the Franciscans established their missions in the area in
the early 1600s.

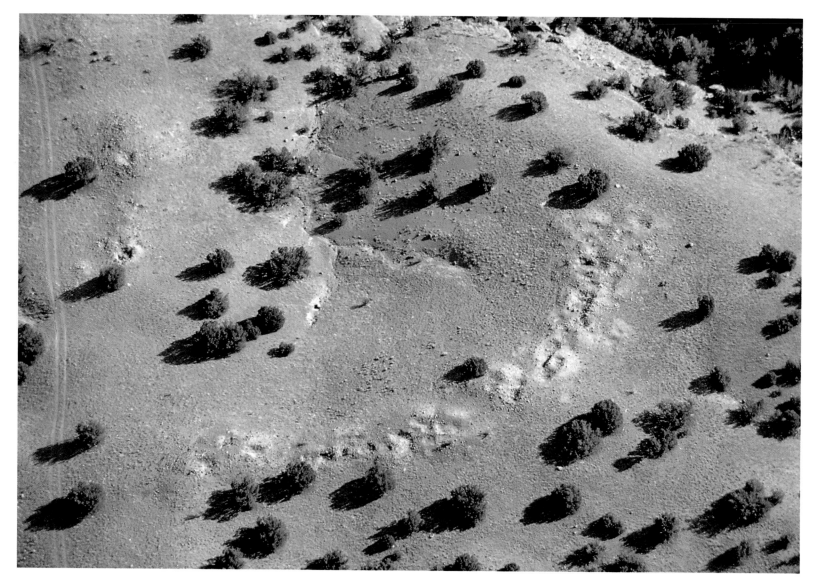

BURNT CORN RUIN, GALISTEO BASIN, NEW MEXICO (A.D. 1200S–1300S?)

Burnt Corn Pueblo is one of the earlier large Galisteo Basin pueblos. The two hundred–room settlement was built atop a ridge in a fishhook shape. At some point during its occupation, the pueblo apparently experienced an extensive fire. Burned corn found there suggested a name for the site.

PUEBLO LARGO, GALISTEO BASIN, NEW MEXICO (EARLY A.D. 1300S–EARLY 1500S)

COMANCHE GAP, GALISTEO BASIN, NEW MEXICO (A.D. 1300S–1600S)

"Comanche Gap" is the name given to the break in a long volcanic dike that slices across the Galisteo Basin. The people who
inhabited the large villages in the Galisteo area from the A.D.
1300s to the 1600s used the Comanche Gap dike and other rocky
outcrops in the area as a medium for their rock art. In different
parts of the basin, rock-art images seem to follow a similar theme.
The long dike at Comanche Gap is dominated by war imagery.
Depicted here are warriors whose shields are covered with stars
and other protective symbols, a woman pregnant with a warrior
child, and Shalakos who act as warriors. These images may have
been designed to impart protective power to the area and especially to serve as warnings to raiding Plains tribes.

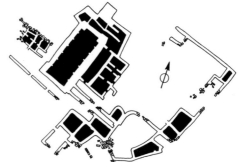

JÉMEZ STATE MONUMENT (GUISEWA), NEW MEXICO (A.D. 1300s–1680)

Guisewa Pueblo is located near Jémez Hot Springs, twelve miles north of modern Jémez Pueblo. A chapel was erected by a Franciscan priest journeying with Oñate's expedition of 1598. In the early 1600s, Guisewa, one of the main Jémez villages, was the seat of the Spanish mission of San José de la Congression. The pueblo was abandoned in 1621, but in 1627 a Spanish priest forced the resettlement of a small number of Jémez people here; the village was finally abandoned after the Pueblo Revolt of 1680. When Adolph Bandelier visited the ruins of Guisewa in the late nineteenth century, he estimated that the pueblo had risen at least two stories, was built around several plazas, and probably housed as many as eight hundred inhabitants.

KWASTIYUKWA, JÉMEZ MOUNTAINS,
NEW MEXICO (A.D. 1300–1700)

Kwastiyukwa, located on a narrow
projecting mesa, was occupied in-
termittently for almost four hundred years. Like other late-
prehistoric pueblos in the Jémez
Mountains, it is situated at an ele-
vation of more than 7,500 feet. Kwastiyukwa is an enormous masonry pueblo with as many as three thousand rooms surrounding
seven plazas. It rose four or five stories high. At the north end of
the site a large depression served as a mortar pit and reservoir. A
row of roomblocks in this area may represent the latest construction interval at the site, dating perhaps to the period of the Spanish Reconquest of 1696.

JÉMEZ RIVER IN SNOW, NEW MEXICO

SAN PEDRO WILDERNESS, NEW MEXICO

KIVA, JÉMEZ MOUNTAINS, NEW MEXICO

GRAN QUIVIRA, SALINAS MONUMENT, NEW MEXICO (A.D. 1300–1670S)

Gran Quivira is one of three archaeological sites that make up Salinas National Monument in central New Mexico. "Salinas" refers
to the remains of a saline lake where salt was procured and traded
in both prehistoric and historic times. Gran Quivira consists of
seventeen house mounds and nine kivas; a Spanish mission dates
to the 1620s. The first Spanish account of Gran Quivira in the
early 1600s reported that it was a large pueblo housing as many as
three thousand people. Disease, drought, and raids by Plains
tribes caused both the Pueblo people and the Spanish to abandon
the settlement during the 1670s.

ABÓ, SALINAS NATIONAL MONUMENT, NEW MEXICO (A.D. 1300–1670S)

Abó was a thriving pueblo when the Spanish first arrived in 1591. Like Gran Quivira, Abó was occupied by speakers of the Tompiro language. The site consists of numerous prehistoric and historic house mounds and the remains of a Spanish mission. Because it was located at the center of a number of trails that connected the Salinas pueblos with the Great Plains to the east and the Rio Grande Valley to the west, Abó was a trading center both before and during Spanish occupation. In the 1670s, Abó was abandoned as both Spanish and Pueblo people moved south to resettle near El Paso.

QUARAI, SALINAS NATIONAL
MONUMENT, NEW MEXICO
(A.D. 1300–1670S)

Quarai was a Tiwa-speaking village, unlike neighboring Abó.
Its masonry roomblocks,
some three stories high, surrounded
at least six plazas. When Adolph
Bandelier visited the site in the late nineteenth century, he estimated that it had once held as many as six hundred people. A mission was established at Quarai in 1628, but the Spanish occupation
of the settlement was short-lived. It was abandoned in 1674.

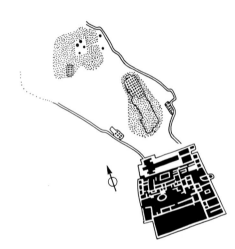

PECOS PUEBLO, PECOS NATIONAL
MONUMENT, NEW MEXICO
(A.D. 1250–1838)

Pecos Pueblo is located near the
junction of Glorietta Arroyo and
the Pecos River. The easternmost
of the Pueblo settlements, prehistoric Pecos was at a gateway be-
tween the Pueblo world and the Great Plains to the east. It served
for centuries as a center of trade. The village that the Coronado
expedition encountered in 1540 was fortress-like. Built on a ridge,
it was a terraced, four-story structure enclosing a large plaza. The
plaza was rimmed by covered corridors on the second and third
stories that allowed residents to walk around the entire pueblo
without touching the ground. At this time, Pecos may have had as
many as two thousand residents. Eventually, the Spanish established a mission, convent, and chapel here, the ruins of which are
still visible. Drought, disease, and raids by other tribes seriously
reduced the population at Pecos and the last remaining residents
moved to Jémez Pueblo in 1838.

128

UPPER PUEBLO, PECOS RIVER, NEW MEXICO

ACOMA PUEBLO, NEW MEXICO (A.D. 1000?–PRESENT)

Acoma occupies a high, steep-sided mesa about sixty miles west
of Albuquerque. The village is one of the oldest continuously occupied communities in the United States, inhabited for perhaps
one thousand years. Acoma experienced sporadic European con-
tact during the mid-1500s and in 1598 Spanish *conquistadores* razed
the village and many residents were enslaved. In 1629, Juan Rami-
rez, a Spanish priest, arrived at Acoma and built the mission
church that still stands at the south end of the village. Where the
people of Acoma lived after their village was destroyed is not
clear, but tree-ring dates recently taken from houses on the mesa
indicate that virtually all were built between 1646 and 1652. Today
Acoma is primarily a ceremonial center. While most families live
in villages below the mesa, virtually all maintain a home in their
ancient city.

SAN FELIPE PUEBLO, NEW MEXICO (A.D. 1300?–PRESENT)

San Felipe Pueblo is located on the west bank of the Rio Grande at the base of Santa Ana Mesa about twenty-five miles north of Albuquerque. It is the central village of the five eastern Keresan-speaking pueblos. Tradition places the origin of the Keresan people to the north of their present location, and it has been suggested that their homeland may have centered on the Chaco Canyon area. The pueblo of San Felipe has apparently shifted location a number of times in the past centuries. When Coronado passed up the Rio Grande Valley in 1540, he noted a pueblo at the foot of La Mesita. Travelers during the 1580s and 1590s found two villages of San Felipe people on either side of the river. In the early 1600s, a Spanish mission was established at Old San Felipe on the east bank of the river. Both villages were abandoned during the Pueblo Revolt. San Felipe people lived for a time in a village atop Santa Ana Mesa, but in 1696 they descended from the mesa and established the present village of San Felipe on the west bank of the Rio Grande. Both sides of the river were used for agriculture, which was the primary means of subsistence for the pueblo until the twentieth century.

HANO–SICHOMOVI–WALPI, FIRST MESA, HOPI, ARIZONA
(A.D. 1680–PRESENT)

First Mesa, one of the three Hopi mesas, is a finger of land that projects south from Black Mesa, an extensive upland area in northeastern Arizona. The three villages perched here—Hano, Sichomovi, and Walpi—were established after the Pueblo Revolt of 1680. Walpi had earlier been located below the mesa, nearer to the spring that provided water for the pueblo. Fear of Spanish reprisals after the revolt led the residents of Walpi to move to their present perch at the very tip of the mesa. Hano (foreground) was established shortly afterward by refugees from the Tewa pueblos of the Rio Grande Valley. They built their village at the head of the trail to the mesa top, a position that provided protection for Walpi. The residents of Hano still speak Tewa in spite of their three hundred–year residence among the Hopi. Sichomovi, the third village, was apparently established sometime during the mid-1700s in a location between Hano and Walpi. Today, few people live in Walpi full-time, but its houses are carefully maintained for use during traditional ceremonies.

136

TAOS PUEBLO, NEW MEXICO (A.D. 1300?–PRESENT)

MOUNTAIN FORM, VILLAGE FORM
Unity in the Pueblo World

By Rina Swentzell

It was midday. I sat next to my great-grandmother, Gia Khuun, against the south adobe wall of our Santa Clara Pueblo house. We sat quietly, listening to the buzzing of flies, when she caught the sound of an airplane in the distant sky. Gia Khuun was rubbing the loose, leathery skin of her hands when she reached for my hand and nodded upwards. I started to speak but she shook my hand to be quiet. The sound grew louder; we caught sight of the vapor trail and watched it disappear over Thunjo, Black Mesa. When the sound died, the buzzing of the flies resumed.

This was forty-five years ago and I was eight years old, yet I still remember the expression on Gia Khuun's face and, mostly, the look in her eyes. She didn't understand. We had never seen an airplane. We saw only vapor trails and heard the rumbling in the sky. What was happening? Cars were a very recent part of our lives. When Gia Khuun first saw the car which my father brought home, she walked around it with her palms out as if to caress, but could never quite touch it. I, on the other hand, nearly leapt onto the backseat. As we drove over the dirt road toward the Pueblo day school and back again, she held onto the door handle and tightly squeezed my leg, holding on. That time, also, I felt her confusion. Jolts of change were rattling her understanding of the world. It was 1947.

Paul Logsdon arrived in New Mexico in 1955, a young military jet pilot in the air force. After twenty-three years of service he retired, in 1976, to begin a second career that would combine his lifelong love of flying with his passion for the Southwest. As an aerial photographer, Logsdon quickly established a reputation with editors, scientists and scholars, advertising agencies, art collectors, and museums. In 1982 he was invited to participate in the New Mexico Photographic Survey, sponsored by the Museum of New Mexico's Museum of Fine Arts.

He flew a Cessna 150, a small plane that he compared to a very tall tripod. It has been said that Logsdon thought of his plane as an extension of himself, something he put on and wore. In much the same way he perceived the universal human past as an extension of himself. His airplane enabled him to both glimpse and participate in the interconnectedness of all life through time.

I never met Paul Logsdon, but when I first saw his photographs at the Museum of Indian Arts and Culture in Santa Fe I was awestruck. To see the Southwest village forms, from the air, within their natural context of hills, valleys, and mountains was very exciting for me, a descendant of those people who created these marvelous places. Feelings stemming from the Pueblo world rushed through me as I walked from photograph to photograph. They reminded me of Pueblo stories which tell us that everything and everybody exists within a context. A house is part of the village form, the village form is part of the hills and mountains, and the whole is part of the universe. I am part of my family, my family is part of the community, and the community is part of the human world, which is part of existence. Logsdon photographed from such a distance that the valley, hill, or mountain forms were captured in their contextual relationship to the human-built villages. The photographs show an exquisite interrelationship of Pueblo/Anasazi–built forms and natural formations in which connectedness and harmony are expressed as goals for human existence.

The photographs repeat for me the Tewa Pueblo belief that all of life is sacred, that the breath of life, the *powaha*, flows through all life expressions—even village forms. *Powaha* translates as water–wind–breath. It is that which energizes all life. It touches and emanates out of rocks, trees, and houses. It is not discriminatory and does not remain exclusively in the human context. The "old ones" did not live according to an elaborate and formalized ideology of absolute truth that set up an all-knowing and powerful God, in the image of man, and one in which only humans were special enough to go to heaven—in the future. They lived knowing that this place, this time, is all that there is, that there is no heaven and no God. This place is where it all happens—happiness, sadness, pain, obligation, responsibility, and joy. Human life, in the traditional Pueblo world, is based on philosophical premises that promote consideration, compassion, and gentleness towards both human and nonhuman beings. In this thinking, every act or thought of any person has an effect on the configuration and feeling of the whole of existence. Rituals, dances, and songs, even today, are about achieving harmony with the life force, the *powaha*, which is experienced in the flow of the water and movement of the wind. It is also understood that the achievement of harmony is transitory since the *powaha* is constant re-creation and transformation. At death, cycles and transformation are honored. In a Tewa song, the dead are entreated not to remember this realm of existence because everything and everybody must change:

Eat the food that now we bring you
And remember us no more!
Give us ample food, and now
No longer we remember you!

Belief in the organic quality of life is vividly expressed in these photographs of ruins, such as Posi-Ouinge, that are but mounds of patterned earth disappearing back into the hills and plateaus. It is very comforting to know that my body will also return into the earth and that my breath will continue into the cosmic breath of life—my specific self not remembering this specific lifetime. The eventual transformation of both physical and spiritual beings into the breath, or life force, was continually reiterated by Gia Khuun who would say, "That is the way it is—we all go back into the earth where we change to join the clouds." Clouds, smoke, and steam: visual expression of the breath.

Accordingly, the old ones did not see human beings as the primary expression of the life force. Life, for them, was not defined in hierarchical terms. They did not see control and power over others as the primary goal of human existence. They taught that humans could derive strength and power from rocks, trees, clouds, and other animals by honoring them in words and action. In fact, animals and natural phenomena were accorded much power in the human world:

> Water-spider spread his legs to the north and to the south, to the west and to the east, and then he said, "Now indeed I have measured it. Here is the center of the earth and here you must build your city!" But the people said, "We have been hunting for the center of the earth a long time, and we wish to be sure." So, they asked Rainbow to measure it also. So the Rainbow stretched his bright arch to the north and to the south, to the west and to the east, measuring the distance. Then he, too, gave his decision: "Here at this place is the heart of the earth" (Carr 1979, 17).

This attitude of the equal status of all life expressions extends also to human-built spaces and structures. As in many cultures, hierarchical structuring of spaces and buildings, such as having the cathedral at the center of a radiating town plan, does not happen in the Pueblo world. Rather, there are unified village forms that include equalitarian units of storage and living spaces. Individual house units are balanced by the communal kiva and plaza spaces. The age-old human dilemma of the individual versus the group is resolved by advocating a balanced interaction of the two. The individual person or house unit cannot be justified without its context of the community or village form, and the community form has no meaning without the individual units. One cannot exist without the other, as the sky cannot exist without the earth or the male without the female entity.

Contexts are important but so are the elements of the whole. When I was a child and our houses were still commonly built by the people of Santa Clara Pueblo, the various parts of the house structure, such as footings, walls, and roof, were fed, blessed, and asked to give their strength to the whole unit. Each element was believed to contain more than inert substances. In a Keres myth, a shaman "struck the north wall of the house, the middle of the wall. There south downward came out water. . . . Again to the west he came and next there in the

SANTA CLARA PUEBLO, NEW MEXICO (A.D. 1300?–PRESENT)

west he struck it. Then there eastward a bear came out" (Boas 1928, 15). The myths, stories, and songs describe a world in which a house or structure is not an object, as such, but part of a cosmological worldview that recognizes multiplicity, simultaneity, inclusiveness, and interconnectedness.

The people, then, are obligated to act respectfully to each element of the house as well as to the whole unit—house or community form. Showing respect includes prayers—talking, to the ground before building, to the walls as they are built, and to the defined interior spaces. Feeding the house or structure and the contained spaces with cornmeal or roots is done periodically thereafter to continually affirm the ongoing relationship. Interconnection with the house is undeniable, since the house has the capability to reject specific human presences within it.

With the belief that places also are alive, Pueblo people visit the old ruins to breathe in the strength of the place and of "those who have gone on before." Gia Khuun said that a place breathes in and incorporates thoughts and feelings of all beings who enter its space. She said that we remain a part of any place we visit—any place where we breathe or leave our sweat. That is why we must think and move carefully wherever we go, because we become one with the place and, therefore, influence its spiritual quality.

These photographs catch the lingering breath or spiritual quality of these places. It seems to me that Paul Logsdon felt that mystical quality when he explained: "I have to figure out how to turn and project myself visually ahead to the spot where I want to be . . . ; there is only one place in the sky where I can get just the picture I want" (Elliott 1986). And, very often, that one place in the sky highlights textures of form, shadow, and line that give a sense of mystery and a feeling of the multiple levels of reality within which Pueblo people live.

Multiple levels of reality include both the physical and spiritual. Physically, our community is at the center of the universe—but so is every other community. There is not one but many truths. Truth is dependent on the context. So it is also with the spiritual world. We are many beings at once. We are not only human. This belief makes communication and interaction with houses, places, plants, and animals possible. One of my great-uncles, for example, was known to howl, to talk, with the coyotes. Other people are known to transform into deer, owls, or coyotes.

Intimacy with the human and natural contexts is essential to operate in the multiple levels of reality. Intimacy with the land, with the earth, is especially crucial. In our myths and stories, the Pueblo cosmos is defined as a contained spherical unit. The male sky is referred to as a basket, while the female earth is a bowl. The basket-sky covers the terraced bowl-earth to complete the spherical world. Within the lower earth-half are the horizontal multilevels, worlds, or four planes of existence, which exist simultaneously. Pueblo people and other living beings emerged into this fourth world at the north opening of the earth mother. That intimate connection and relationship with the mother pervades all thought and action.

Inclusiveness, then, is a value strongly embraced. Opposites, such as sky and earth, light and heavy, male and female, warm and cold, are seen as essential parts of the contained spherical Pueblo world-unit. The idea of the containment of opposites within the inclusive whole is in alignment with the universal Pueblo concept of simultaneity within which many levels of existence are recognized. Opposites are necessary to define a healthy whole. Logsdon's photographs, taken from the male sky by a man in a phallic-shaped machine, wonderfully capture the soft, round community and kiva shapes that symbolize the womb of the female earth. It is Logsdon as the opposite giving us a view that is impossible from only the female earth.

These opposites or dualities also create tension and are the source of movement and continual transformation. All life forms, including man and woman, as opposites, create life in their union. Winter and Summer, as the social/political organizing principle of the Tewa Pueblos, assure psychical and political movement within the human context. Each equinox, the Winter group, which consists of approximately half of the members of the community, takes or gives the decision-making power to the Summer people. Stasis is avoided.

Archaeological work, especially in the Chama Basin area, shows that during pre-Contact years the average length of stay at one site was twelve to twenty-five years. The vast number of sites, many recorded by Logsdon over the course of the thirteen years he photographed here, would indicate that the Pueblo people engaged in continuous movement on the land. The scattered house units and unified village forms were places through which the people moved. They did not settle in one place for a long time, but rather emulated the movement of the seasons, wind, clouds, and life cycles by moving frequently. They responded to the movement of floods, droughts, and social tensions. The movement of the clouds told them how they should move on the ground. Their sense of "home" was in the space between the earth and the sky and not within specific human constructions.

Logsdon's photographs show the settling of the people alongside waterways, springs, or within valleys and on mesas and plateaus. They settled where they could meet their physical and spiritual needs. As they took from the land, they were obligated to give something back in return. It could be thoughts of thankfulness or a sprinkle of cornmeal, symbolic of nourishment and recognition. Shrines and other special places of connection were built where people could leave offerings. Petroglyphs and pictographs recorded the multiple levels of interaction between people and other natural forces.

The patterning of human villages within the canyons, mesas, and mountains, so abundantly and beautifully shown in Logsdon's photographs, is but one element of the entire living and gathering space of the Pueblo world. Also important are the many points of interaction via shrines and nonarchitectural gathering places within the natural landscape and that are often some distance from the village. The hills and mountains are boundaries of the horizontal world space. The six directions (north, west, south, east, up, and down) define the outer perimeters of the world-sphere. The primacy of the six-direction system and the color associations for the Tewa world are illustrated in this prayer:

> Here and now we bring you, O our old ones,
> Sun fire deity and Blue Cloud person of the North,
> Sun fire deity and Yellow Cloud person of the West,
> Sun fire deity and Red Cloud person of the South,
> Sun fire deity and White Cloud person of the East,
> Sun fire deity and Dark person of the below,
> Sun fire deity and All-colored person of the above,
> Here we bring you now our special prayer stick,
> We make for you an offering of sacred meal.

For Logsdon, the forces of nature are a ravager against which ancient walls must struggle. In his poem "Trementina" he makes clear a mind-set at odds with Pueblo thought:

> It stands alone
> below the rim
> struggling mightily against earth enemy.
>
> Wind, rain
> and humankind
> have worked their smothering spell

A vagrant wall
thrusts mighty shoulders
and earth is broken and revealing.

It is not a gentle dying into but a mighty struggle against organicism and transformation. Many cultures have given themselves to the impulse to overcome movement and death. The ancient Egyptians, for example, struggled against inevitable natural forces by building pyramids as ladders into the sky so the entombed dead could easily travel to the above. This idea is foreign to Pueblo thought, as is the image of "a vagrant wall."

In the Pueblo, walls are alive and participate in contexts and cycles of life and death. They are never vagrant. As a child, I was once worried about the cracks forming in the wall of a house at Santa Clara Pueblo. For days I watched the cracks widening. Finally, I asked Gia Khuun why the people living in the house were not fixing the wall. She explained that the house had endured for a long time as a good house, and that it was time for it to die. It needed a rest before it was built up again. As predicted, the house fell down and the mud from which it was made was remixed with water and used to raise up other walls in its place. In this way, the earth strengthened the village.

WORKS CITED

Boas, Franz. 1928. *Keresan Texts*. New York: The American Ethnological Society.
Carr, Pat. 1979. *Mimbres Mythology*. El Paso: University of Texas Press.
Elliott, Malinda. 1986. "Camera in the Sky." *Americana* 14:4.

ABOUT THE CONTRIBUTORS

Stephen Lekson, Ph.D., is an archaeologist, author, and president of the Crow Canyon Archaeological Center in Denver.

Rina Swentzell, Ph.D., is an architectural historian and educational consultant. She is a member of Santa Clara Pueblo.

Catherine M. Cameron, Ph.D., is an archaeologist on the staff of the Advisory Council on Historic Preservation.

John E. Lobdell, Ph.D., is a bioarchaeologist and environmental scientist who has worked in the Arctic, Subarctic, Northwest Coast, Southwest, and Great Plains.